INSULTS & COMEBACKS: WORK EDITION

Universal Comebacks for Work Woes

Jax Joust

Published by Lazy Cotton Press

PREFACE

Welcome back, stalwarts of the stinging comeback, to the newest volume of our verbal arsenal—specifically tailored for the work arena. Veterans of our series will recognize the shield of audacity and the rapier of repartee. Newcomers, prepare to discover that sometimes, the pen is not just mightier, but also more biting than the sword.

This book is your savvy compendium for the corporate jungle, where skirmishes unfold in boardrooms and cubicles, not trenches. Here, we arm you against the overbearing client, the micro-managing boss, the invariably "right" customer, and their ilk—those who test our patience and expect silent, smiling endurance.

No longer. This guide offers you the tools to navigate these trials with grace and a well-placed barb. It's the companion for when the high road is blocked, and the only option is to stand firm, wits at the ready.

We're not here to incite discourtesy but to be prepared when it intrudes, to quench its flames with a well-aimed phrase. Ready yourself for laughter, recognition, and an arsenal of retorts so sharp they'll slice through pomposity with precision.

With a quip and a wink,

Jax Joust
2301 Lady Bug Drive, New York NY
2023

CONTENT

1 - "The Scope Creepers: When Clients Want More for Less" — 1

2 - "The 'Just Part of Your Job' Jokers" — 12

3 - "The Backseat Experts: Clients Who Know 'Better'" — 23

4 - "The Procrastinating Payers: Chasing the Elusive Check" — 34

5 - "The Micromanaging Managers: Overseeing Overly Close Oversight" — 45

6 - "The Bargain Hunters: Customers with Unrealistic Expectations" — 56

7 - "The Indecisive Client Conundrum: Decision-Making Dilemmas" — 67

8 - "The 'Urgent' Illusionists: Last-Minute Mayhem Makers" — 78

9 - "The Feedback Fanatics: Critique Without Construct" 89

10 - "The 'I'm Never Wrong' Patrons: Handling the Infallible" 100

1 - "The Scope Creepers: When Clients Want More for Less"

This chapter is for those times when your boss is so close you can tell what they had for lunch. Comebacks that help you assert your competence without risking your job.

"More work without more pay? What a concept! Let's try 'less client' without 'less headache'."

"I love charity work, especially when it's involuntary and for profit-making businesses."

"You want extras? Sure, let me just check with my landlord if I can pay rent with your gratitude."

"Add-ons without pay? I'll send my extra bills to your home address then."

"You want a freebie? Let me introduce you to a groundbreaking concept called 'paying for services'."

"Unpaid extra work? Oh, I must have missed that fairy tale in economics class."

"I'll start working for exposure the day my mortgage accepts it as payment."

"More for less? Sure, let me just downgrade your project to 'thoughts and prayers' status."

"You want a bonus track when you haven't paid for the album? Fascinating."

"I'll consider your request for a moment... Okay, moment's over."

2 - "The 'Just Part of Your Job' Jokers"

For when coworkers turn into unasked-for career coaches, this chapter offers comebacks to gently remind them that you didn't sign up for their mentorship program.

"Oh, it's part of my job? Must've missed that in the fine print where it said I'm also a genie with unlimited wishes."

"Sure, I'll add that to my job description, right after 'professional unicorn trainer'."

"Part of my job? So is breathing, but you don't see me charging extra for that."

"I'll get right on that, just after I finish my other duties as the company's astronaut."

"If doing everything was part of the job, they wouldn't need anyone else. But here you are."

"Let me check my job description. Nope, 'miracle worker' isn't listed."

"I'd agree with you, but then we'd both be wrong about what my job is."

"Part of my job? So is avoiding tasks that aren't, like this one."

"I'll pencil that in between 'telepath' and 'time traveler'."

"Sure, and while I'm at it, I'll also assume my role as the office psychic."

3 - "The Backseat Experts: Clients Who Know 'Better'"

When someone tries to hijack your hard work, this chapter provides the verbal judo you need to take back credit without breaking a sweat.

"You know better? Fantastic. I'll send over my tasks and you can show me how it's done."

"Your expertise is so vast, I'm surprised you don't have my job. Oh wait, you don't."

"You're so knowledgeable, why don't you take over and I'll just bill you for the pleasure?"

"You've got so much input, I'm starting to think you don't need me at all. Shall I leave?"

"You must be so exhausted carrying all that wisdom around. Want to put it down and let me work?"

"Oh, you used to do my job? Great, you can also do the time travel to when that was relevant."

"I'm thrilled you've watched a YouTube tutorial, but I'll stick to my decade of experience, thanks."

"Your unsolicited advice is like a screen door on a submarine—unnecessary and ineffective."

"You have a suggestion? Hold on, let me get my 'I couldn't care less' notebook."

"You're right, you do know better—how to annoy me into productivity."

4 - "The Procrastinating Payers: Chasing the Elusive Check"

For every time someone turns a meeting into a monologue, here's how to steer the conversation back without commandeering the ship.

"Your payment is playing hide and seek. Spoiler: it's winning."

"I've seen glaciers move faster than your payments."

"Your check must be a ninja because it's got some serious stealth skills."

"I'd say your payment is late, but that would imply it's actually coming."

"You treat payment deadlines like recommendations. They're not."

"I'll start a new hobby while I wait for your payment: aging."

"Your payment's so slow,
I'm starting to think it's a piece of
performance art."

"I'd call to remind you about the payment, but I don't want to interrupt its hibernation."

"If I had a dollar for every late payment, oh wait, I should, shouldn't I?"

"Your payment's like a unicorn, often discussed but never seen."

5 - "The Micromanaging Managers: Overseeing Overly Close Oversight"

When a coworker confuses your job description with theirs, this chapter offers comebacks to push the workload back where it belongs.

"If I wanted someone to breathe down my neck, I would've worked at a scarf shop."

"Your micromanaging is so intense, I'm starting to think you're my new skin."

"You're so close I can tell what you had for breakfast. Personal space, ever heard of it?"

"You must have a lot of free time to spend it all watching me work."

"If you micromanage any harder, you'll need to be listed as a co-author on my tasks."

"I was going to take initiative,
but I see you've rented out the space."

"With your level of oversight,
I'm surprised you don't just do the job
yourself."

"You're like a GPS for work—constantly recalculating but never taking the wheel."

"I'd ask for some autonomy, but I'm not sure you'd approve the request."

"You've got a talent for micromanaging. Ever considered a career in puppeteering?"

6 - "The Bargain Hunters: Customers with Unrealistic Expectations"

Climbing the corporate ladder is hard enough without backstabbers. This chapter helps you address the rivalry with wit and keep your rivals at bay.

"You want five-star service at a one-star price? Let me introduce you to the concept of 'math'."

"Your budget says 'economy',
but your expectations scream 'luxury'.
Something's gotta give."

"You're hunting for a bargain? This isn't a yard sale, and my services aren't second-hand."

"You want a discount? Sure, let me just discount the effort I put into my work too."

"A bargain? Sure, if by 'bargain' you mean paying full price for quality work."

"You expect a discount just for showing up? This isn't a game show."

"Your desire for a deal is only matched by my desire to pay my bills. Funny how that works."

"You want premium work for a clearance price? What a fantasy!"

"I'll throw in a discount the day my landlord throws in free rent."

"You want a bargain? I want a vacation. Guess which one's happening first?"

7 - "The Indecisive Client Conundrum: Decision-Making Dilemmas"

Every office has doom-and-gloomers. This chapter is full of comebacks to lighten the mood and maybe even crack a smile on the most stoic of faces.

"Your indecision is like a software update in the middle of my workday—unnecessary and time-consuming."

"You change your mind more often than I change my passwords."

"If you were any more indecisive, you'd be a 'maybe' button on a survey."

"You've got a talent for indecision. Ever thought of going pro?"

"Your decision-making skills are so rare, they're almost mythical."

"I've seen waffles less flip-floppy than your decisions."

"You're not indecisive, you're decisionally challenged."

"If I had a dime for every time you changed your mind, I'd be on a yacht, not on this call."

"Your indecision is giving me whiplash."

"You're the Hamlet of clients. To decide or not to decide, that is the question."

8 - "The 'Urgent' Illusionists: Last-Minute Mayhem Makers"

For the close-talkers and over-the-shoulder readers, here's how to set personal boundaries with comebacks that are firm but fair.

"Your emergency planning is so poor, it's almost an emergency itself."

"You've got a real talent for turning nothing into a five-alarm fire."

"Urgent for you, apparently,
means 'I forgot to do my part on time'."

"Your lack of planning does not constitute an 'urgent' situation on my end."

"You treat the word 'urgent' like it's a seasoning—sprinkle it on everything."

"I'll add your 'urgent' request to the queue. It's right behind 'impossible' and ahead of 'inconceivable'."

"You say 'urgent', I hear 'I didn't think this through'."

"Your urgency is as convincing as a toddler's promise to be good."

"You have an 'urgent' request? Join the club. Meetings are on Thursdays, bring snacks."

"Another 'urgent' task? Let me just finish up curing world hunger first."

9 - "The Feedback Fanatics: Critique Without Construct"

When colleagues think your time is their time, this chapter gives you the words to take back your clock.

"Your feedback is like a screen door on a submarine—full of holes and not very useful."

"If I wanted to be judged without any constructive input, I'd have gone on a reality TV show."

"Your criticism is so vague, it's almost avant-garde."

"You give feedback like a bad movie review—lots of opinions, zero substance."

"Your 'constructive criticism' has about as much structure as a house of cards."

"I appreciate your feedback like I appreciate a headache."

"You have a gift for criticism.
Too bad it's not returnable."

"Your feedback is as helpful as a chocolate teapot."

"Thanks for the critique. I'll file it right between 'useless' and 'ignored'."

"Your feedback is so empty, it echoes."

10 - "The 'I'm Never Wrong' Patrons: Handling the Infallible"

Doubt can be a healthy part of business, but not when it's all you hear. This chapter provides comebacks for when you need to turn skepticism into support.

"You're never wrong? Must be nice living in that fantasy."

"You've never made a mistake? What's it like walking on water?"

"You're always right? I'll alert the media."

"Never wrong? I guess you've never been married then."

"Your track record for being right is as spotless as a toddler's shirt at dinner time."

"You're never wrong. And I'm the Queen of England."

"You're not wrong? Well, there's a first time for everything."

"You're never wrong? Tell me, does that come with a cape or just the usual delusions?"

"You're always right? I'm sure your imaginary friends are impressed."

"Never wrong? I guess you don't need GPS, because you never take a wrong turn."

EPILOGUE

As we close the cover on this latest chapter of our ongoing saga, I hope you feel a renewed sense of readiness—a readiness to face down the daily dragons of the workplace with a fortified spirit and a quiver full of retorts.

Throughout these pages, we've danced a delicate tango with decorum and defiance, learning when to parry with politeness and when to thrust with tenacity. You've been equipped with an arsenal that, if used judiciously, will ensure you're no one's verbal doormat.

But let us not forget that with great wit comes great responsibility. These comebacks are not grenades to be lobbed carelessly into crowds but rather precision tools to be used at the right moment, for the right reasons. Our goal is never to wound but to assert our worth, to draw boundaries, and to demand the respect we deserve.

As you return to the trenches of your daily grind, carry these words with you not as weapons, but as shields. Let them serve as a reminder that while the world may not always be kind, you have the strength, the smarts, and the savvy to navigate it with your head held high and your sense of self intact.

Until we meet again in the pages of our next adventure, may your wit remain as sharp as your resolve, and may your days be as fulfilling as they are free from folly.

With respect and a rye smile,

Jax Joust
2023

© 2023 by Lazy Cotton

All rights reserved. No part of this publication may be reproduced, distributed, or transmitted in any form or by any means, including photocopying, recording, or other electronic or mechanical methods, without the prior written permission of the author, except in the case of brief quotations embodied in critical reviews and certain other noncommercial uses permitted by copyright law.

First Edition

Published by Lazy Cotton Press
www.lazycotton.press

Published by Lazy Cotton Press
www.lazycotton.press

Printed in Great Britain
by Amazon